INSIDE  THE ARMY RANGERS

HOWARD PHILLIPS

PowerKiDS press

NEW YORK

Library of Congress Cataloging-in-Publication Data

Names: Phillips, Howard, 1971- author.
Title: Inside the Army Rangers / Howard Phillips.
Description: New York : PowerKids Press, [2022]. | Series: U.S. Special Ops Forces | Includes index.
Identifiers: LCCN 2020057279 | ISBN 9781725328914 (library binding) | ISBN 9781725328891 (paperback) | ISBN 9781725328907 (6 pack)
Subjects: LCSH: United States. Army. Ranger Regiment, 75th–History–Juvenile literature. | United States. Army–Commando troops–Juvenile literature. | Special forces (Military science)–United States–Juvenile literature.
Classification: LCC UA34.R36 P45 2022 | DDC 356/.1670973–dc23
LC record available at https://lccn.loc.gov/2020057279

Manufactured in the United States of America

CPSIA Compliance Information: Batch #BSPK22. For further information contact Rosen Publishing, New York, New York at 1-800-237-9932.

Find us on 

CONTENTS

On June 6, 1944, **Allied** troops **invaded** France to free it from German forces. During this battle on a beach in Normandy, the troops' **mission** was to climb the nearby cliffs and fight the German army positioned there. An American general, realizing the ascent was going to be difficult, is believed to have said to a group of Army Rangers, "Rangers, lead the way!"

The U.S. Rangers are a group of **elite**, special operations soldiers. They are called upon to do jobs too tough for other soldiers. The Rangers are always ready for combat, and they're often the first to rush into danger.

THIS PAINTING DEPICTS AMERICAN
TROOPS LANDING ON OMAHA BEACH
ON JUNE 6, 1944.

5

During the Middle Ages, a group of soldiers called Rangers served the English king. They protected forest animals from illegal hunters and drove away outlaws.

Native Americans lived throughout North America when British colonists arrived in the 1600s and 1700s. Fights often broke out between them. Native Americans didn't fight like other enemies the British knew. They attacked swiftly and then scattered. British colonists needed a new type of soldier to stop Native American raids. These soldiers needed to know how to survive in the unexplored areas of the wild and be tough and fast.

CHURCH'S RANGERS

THE FIRST GROUP OF AMERICAN RANGERS WAS ORGANIZED BY CAPTAIN BENJAMIN CHURCH IN 1670. THESE MEN USED THE NATIVE AMERICANS' FIGHTING STYLE TO FIND AND KILL A WAMPANOAG CHIEF THEY CALLED KING PHILIP. THEY SPENT LONG PERIODS OF TIME "RANGING," OR QUIETLY SEARCHING, FOR HIM. THIS IS HOW MODERN RANGERS GOT THEIR NAME.

THIS DRAWING OF KING PHILIP'S WAR BETWEEN NATIVE AMERICANS AND COLONISTS APPEARED IN THE 1810 BOOK *HISTORY OF THE DISCOVERY OF AMERICA* BY HENRY TRUMBULL.

The French and Indian War (1754–1763) was a battle between the British and French, as well as their Native American allies. The British army formed groups of Rangers to protect the colonies. These Rangers also helped attack the French.

One of the earliest Ranger groups was named "Rogers's Rangers" after its leader, Major Robert Rogers. He led his men through hundreds of miles of wilderness to raid a Native American village in Quebec, Canada. The ability to attack deep inside enemy territory without being discovered was important for these early Rangers. It's still important for today's U.S. Army Rangers.

RANGERS OF THE AMERICAN REVOLUTION

DURING THE AMERICAN REVOLUTION (1775-1783), RANGER UNITS WERE PUT TOGETHER TO HELP THE CONTINENTAL ARMY FIGHT THE BRITISH. FRANCIS MARION, A MILITARY OFFICER ALSO KNOWN AS THE "SWAMP FOX," LED A GROUP OF RANGERS IN SOUTH CAROLINA. MARION HAD LEARNED **GUERRILLA** TACTICS DURING BATTLES WITH CHEROKEE INDIANS DURING THE FRENCH AND INDIAN WAR. HE USED THESE TACTICS TO SNEAK UP ON BRITISH FORCES AND DEFEAT THEM.

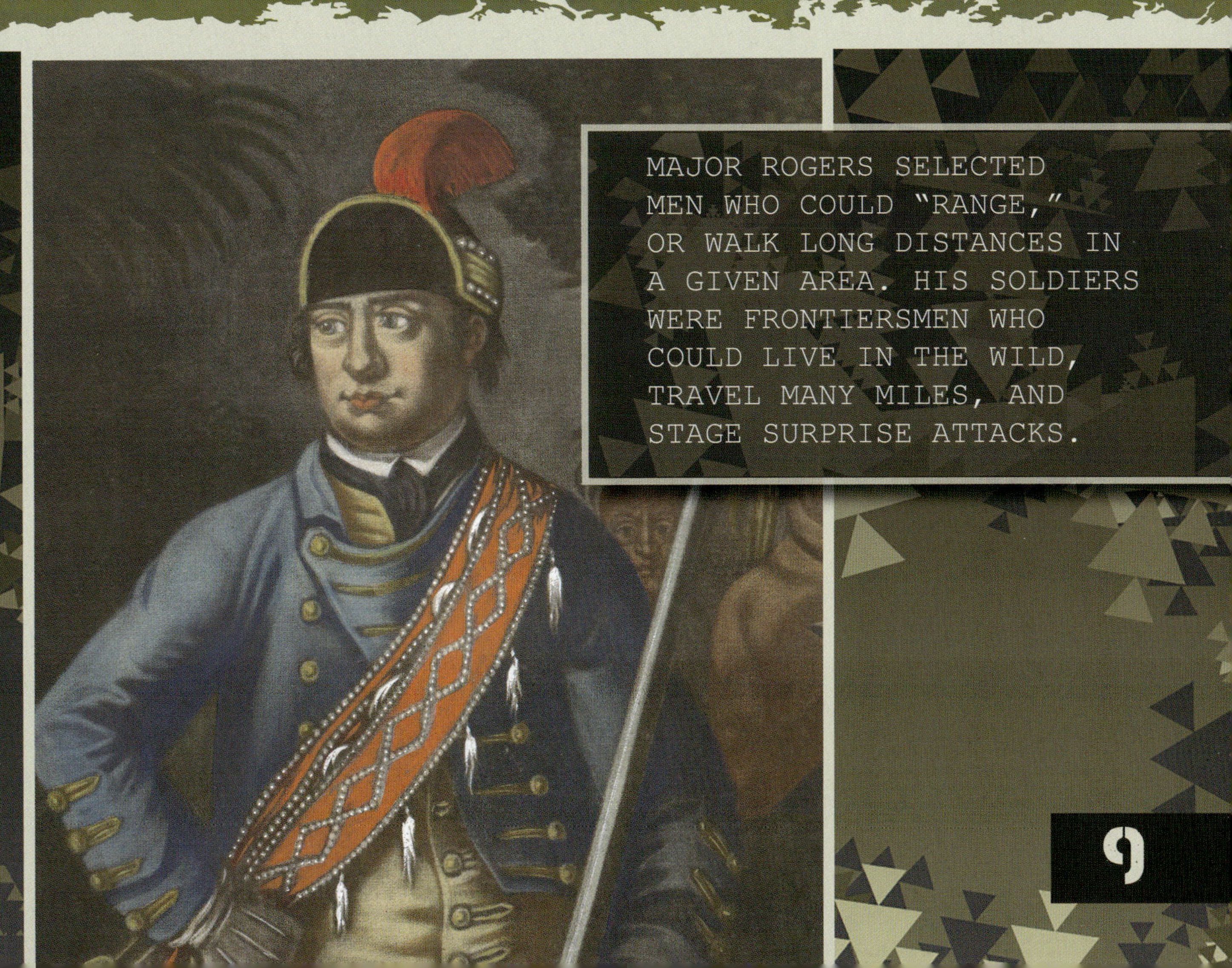

MAJOR ROGERS SELECTED MEN WHO COULD "RANGE," OR WALK LONG DISTANCES IN A GIVEN AREA. HIS SOLDIERS WERE FRONTIERSMEN WHO COULD LIVE IN THE WILD, TRAVEL MANY MILES, AND STAGE SURPRISE ATTACKS.

THE AMERICAN CIVIL WAR

The American Civil War (1861–1865) was a conflict between the Northern (Union) and Southern (Confederate) states. Both sides **recruited** men for Ranger units to carry out **covert** missions. One of the most famous Confederate Ranger units was Mosby's Rangers.

Led by John Singleton Mosby, Mosby's Rangers had success raiding deep behind Union lines, passing thousands of soldiers unnoticed. In 1863, Mosby's Rangers tried to capture an officer from his headquarters in Virginia. Although they didn't find the man they wanted, they were able to capture a general, many soldiers, and a large number of horses.

RANGERS ALSO WORKED TO CUT OFF SUPPLY LINES. THIS MADE IT DIFFICULT FOR THE OTHER SIDE TO SUPPLY ITS TROOPS WITH FOOD AND OTHER MATERIALS NEEDED TO FIGHT THE WAR.

JOHN S. MOSBY

Ranger units were not assembled again until World War II (1939–1945). The U.S. Army Ranger units were made up of army **volunteers**. Their training was based on that of British **Commandos**. The specially skilled soldiers had been fighting in the war since it began. Their experiences with the German army were used in training the U.S. Rangers.

In addition to "leading the way" in France on D-Day in 1944, the Rangers helped invade North Africa in 1942 and Italy in 1943. They also fought in Asia against the Japanese. Today, Rangers continue to travel the world to complete many missions.

MERRILL'S MARAUDERS

MERRILL'S MARAUDERS WERE A GROUP OF U.S. ARMY
RANGERS WHO FOUGHT IN SOUTHEAST ASIA DURING WORLD
WAR II. THEY WERE NAMED FOR THEIR LEADER, FRANK
MERRILL. THE MARAUDERS' MISSION WAS TO CUT OFF
JAPANESE COMMUNICATIONS AND SUPPLY LINES. THEY
BATTLED JAPANESE FORCES WHILE WALKING MORE THAN
1,000 MILES (1,609 KM).

THIS PHOTOGRAPH FROM
1944 SHOWS MERRILL'S
MARAUDERS RANGING IN
THE JUNGLES OF ASIA.
THEY OFTEN JOINED
FORCES FROM CHINA
AND BURMA (MYANMAR).

13

RANGERS IN VIETNAM

During the Vietnam War (1954–1974), the U.S. Army needed a group of soldiers for long-range patrols. These soldiers needed to stay behind enemy lines for long periods of time. They spent most of their time completing **reconnaissance** missions to discover enemy positions.

At first, these long-range patrol units weren't called Rangers. However, their missions and abilities were very much like the Ranger units from earlier wars, such as Mosby's Rangers and Merrill's Marauders. These long-range patrol units eventually became part of Ranger units already fighting in Vietnam. The 1st Ranger **Battalion** of the 75th Ranger Regiment was officially founded in 1974.

THE 75TH

ON JANUARY 1, 1969, THE 75TH RANGER REGIMENT WAS ORGANIZED, AND IT BECAME THE PARENT REGIMENT FOR ALL OTHER RANGER COMPANIES. FIFTEEN RANGER COMPANIES WERE ESTABLISHED UNDER THE 75TH REGIMENT. THIRTEEN OF THESE GROUPS SAW COMBAT DURING THE VIETNAM WAR. AFTER THE WAR, THE 75TH REGIMENT BECAME THE 1ST BATTALION, 75TH INFANTRY. TODAY, THIS ELITE FORCE STILL HELPS PROTECT PEOPLE AROUND THE WORLD.

U.S. SOLDIERS IN VIETNAM USE A HAND-CRANK GENERATOR TO POWER THEIR RADIO EQUIPMENT. SPECIAL OPS UNITS USED RADIOS LIKE THESE TO REPORT TO THEIR COMMANDERS.

REGIMENTS AND BATTALIONS

The 75th Ranger Regiment is still the main group under which the U.S. Army Rangers are organized. Today, this regiment is made up of five battalions, and each battalion is made up of no more than 580 soldiers, including riflemen and support staff.

U.S. Army Rangers have missions that require them to be able to operate both day and night, during any type of weather, and on any kind of **terrain**. Rangers are trained to capture enemies and enemy-held territory. Rangers are also trained for reconnaissance. They know how to complete missions quickly, quietly, and effectively.

THE REGIMENTAL MILITARY INTELLIGENCE BATTALION (RMIB) IS THE FIFTH AND NEWEST BATTALION. ESTABLISHED IN 2017, THE RMIB HELPS RECRUIT AND TRAIN RANGERS.

RSTB

THE RANGERS SPECIAL TROOPS BATTALION, OR RSTB, IS THE FOURTH BATTALION IN THE 75TH RANGER REGIMENT. FORMED IN 2006, THE RSTB HELPS THE FIRST THREE RANGER BATTALIONS AS WELL AS OTHER MILITARY UNITS. IT GIVES COMMUNICATIONS AND RECONNAISSANCE SUPPORT. THE RSTB RECRUITS AND TRAINS SOLDIERS WHO WANT TO BECOME ARMY RANGERS.

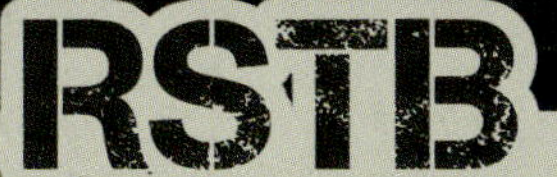

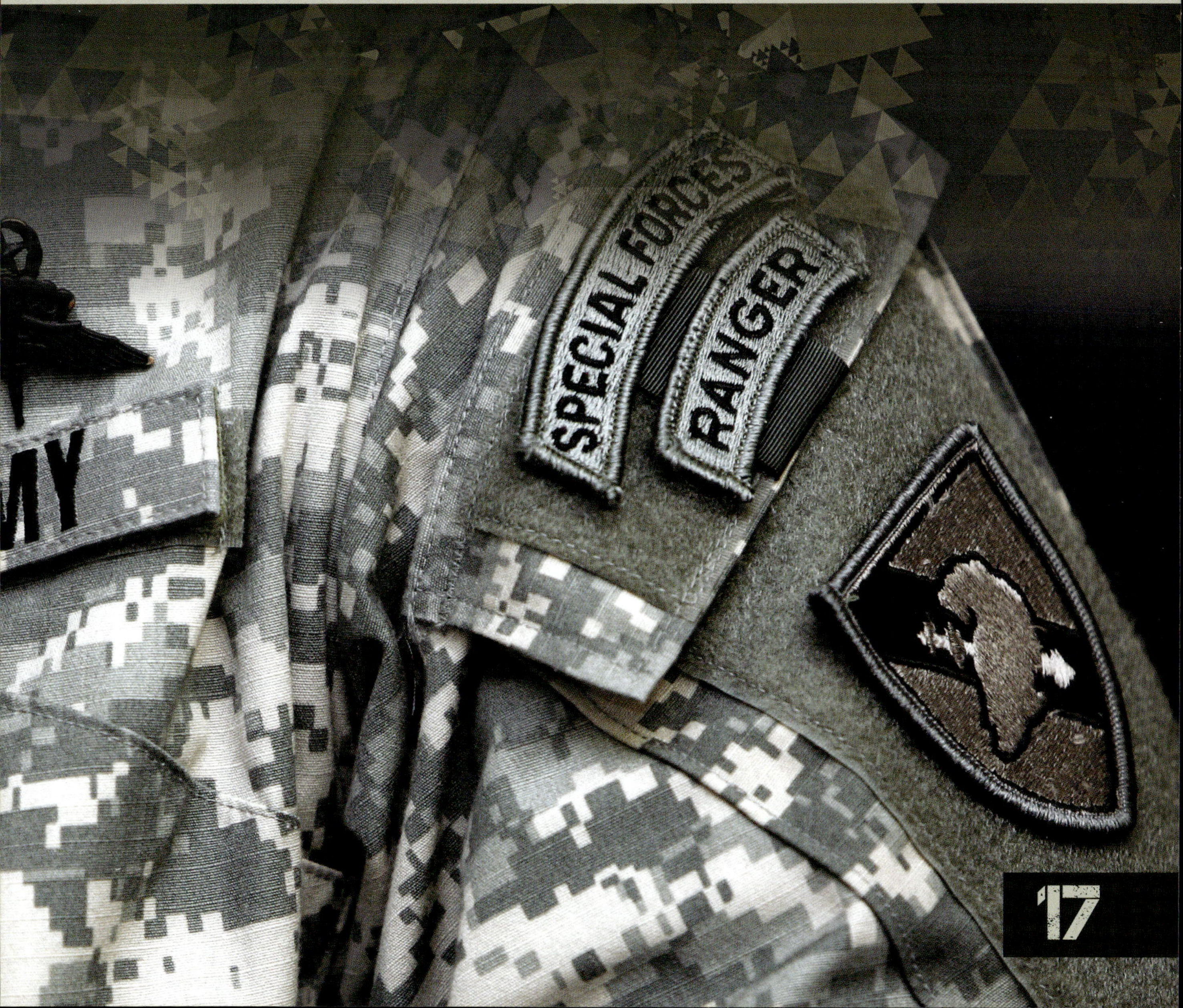

EARNING THE TAN BERET

There are three phases, or stages, of training that most recruits must go through to join the 75th Ranger Regiment. However, before this training, each recruit must first complete the Ranger Assessment and Selection Program, or RASP.

RASP not only teaches the basic skills necessary to be a Ranger but also makes certain the recruit has the physical and mental toughness needed to be a U.S. Army Ranger. All recruits must pass Airborne School. This includes, most importantly, successfully parachuting from an airplane. Rangers are also taught and tested on first aid and advanced life-saving procedures.

RANGERS EARN THE RIGHT TO WEAR A TAN
BERET, WHICH IS THE SPECIAL HAT ONLY
U.S. ARMY RANGERS ARE ALLOWED TO WEAR.

Ranger training is broken down into three phases, or parts. The first phase takes place at Fort Benning, Georgia, and lasts about 20 days. During this period, recruits complete physically exhausting tasks such as obstacle courses, sit-ups, push-ups, and long marches.

The second phase is the 20-day mountain phase. During this time, recruits must work together in small groups in rugged mountain terrain while getting little sleep and eating little. The final stage teaches recruits how to operate in swamps and jungles as well as exercise leadership skills. This phase takes place in Florida and lasts 16 days.

WOMEN RANGERS

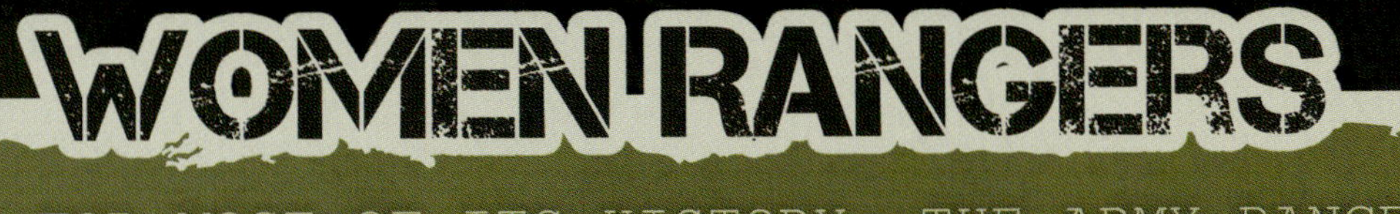

FOR MOST OF ITS HISTORY, THE ARMY RANGERS HAS BEEN A GROUP MADE UP OF MEN ONLY. THIS CHANGED IN 2015 WHEN THE FIRST TWO WOMEN, KRISTEN GRIEST AND SHAYE HAVER, PASSED THE DIFFICULT TRAINING PROCESS. SINCE THEN, MORE THAN 30 WOMEN HAVE BECOME ARMY RANGERS. IN 2019, JANINA SIMMONS BECAME THE FIRST AFRICAN AMERICAN WOMAN TO BECOME A RANGER.

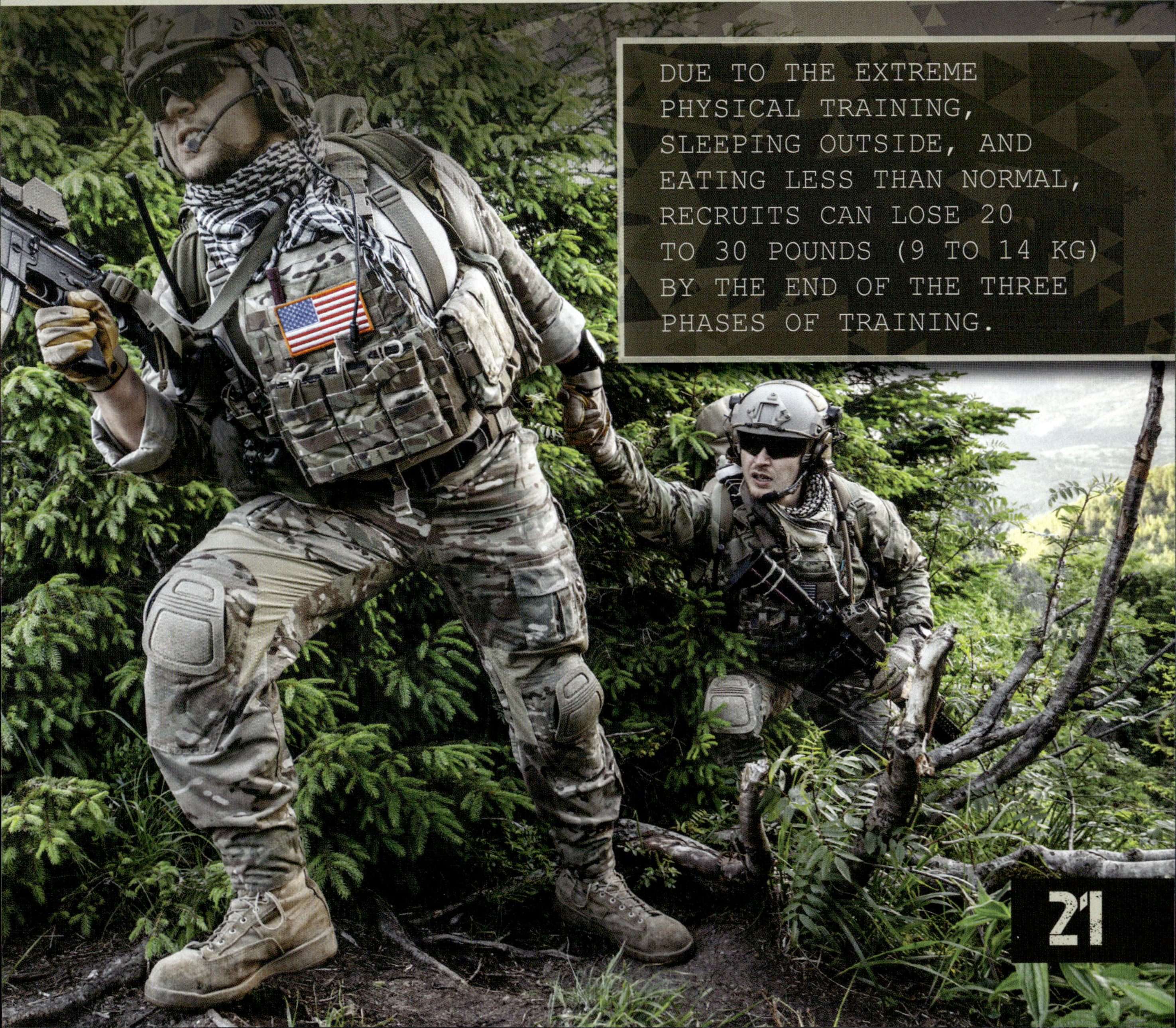

DUE TO THE EXTREME PHYSICAL TRAINING, SLEEPING OUTSIDE, AND EATING LESS THAN NORMAL, RECRUITS CAN LOSE 20 TO 30 POUNDS (9 TO 14 KG) BY THE END OF THE THREE PHASES OF TRAINING.

RANGER
TRAVEL

Each Ranger mission is approached differently. Rangers perform missions all over the world in many kinds of terrain. Rangers reach the area where they will perform their mission in different ways, depending on where it will take place. They may parachute from airplanes. Rangers also use small rubber boats to travel to locations.

Another common way to travel to a mission start area is by helicopter. Rangers slide down to the ground using a special rope. However, once the Rangers reach their start location, they march to complete their mission. A single mission may include many miles of marching to reach the final location.

ONE BATTALION IS ALWAYS READY TO GO
ANYWHERE IN THE WORLD WITHIN 18 HOURS.
FOR 13 WEEKS, ONE RANGER BATTALION IS
READY WITH ALL WEAPONS AND SUPPLIES NECESSARY
FOR A MISSION. AFTER THAT 13-WEEK PERIOD,
IT'S THE NEXT BATTALION'S TURN TO BE READY.

RANGER TOOLS

Army Ranger missions are often covert. They often perform missions on foot after they reach a certain area. They must carry all their gear with them. Most Rangers carry a lightweight but powerful rifle called an M4A1 Carbine. Some carry machine guns for times when extra firepower is needed.

When the Rangers need to hit targets too large or well armored for the M4A1, they have more powerful weapons they can use. Against targets on the ground, they use the Ranger Antitank Weapons System, or RAWS. The RAWS can fire many rounds at a time.

SNIPERS ARE SOLDIERS WHO ARE ABLE TO SHOOT VERY WELL FROM A GREAT DISTANCE WITHOUT BEING NOTICED BY THE ENEMY. RANGER SNIPERS USE A SPECIAL RIFLE THAT CAN HIT TARGETS MORE THAN A MILE (1.6 KM) AWAY.

25

STILL FIGHTING

The U.S. Army Rangers have participated in modern conflicts involving the United States. In 1993, a unit of Rangers was sent to Somalia as part of a military force working to bring peace to the country.

In October 1993, the Rangers undertook a mission to capture several Somali warlords. During the mission, the warlords' soldiers shot down two U.S. helicopters, killing several Rangers. More Rangers were sent in to rescue the survivors. For nearly 18 hours, they fought Somali soldiers. About 600 Somali soldiers died. The Rangers lost six soldiers in the conflict.

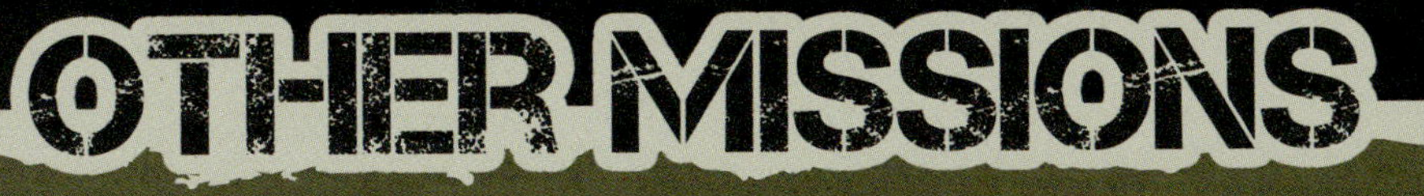

OTHER MISSIONS

IN OCTOBER 2001, THE 3RD BATTALION SUCCESSFULLY
CONDUCTED AN AIRBORNE ASSAULT TO SEIZE AN
AIRFIELD AS PART OF OPERATION ENDURING FREEDOM
IN AFGHANISTAN. MARCH 2003 FOUND THE 3RD
BATTALION LEADING THE WAY BY COMPLETING THE FIRST
AIRBORNE ASSAULT DURING OPERATION IRAQI FREEDOM.
TODAY, THE RANGERS STILL HELP COMBAT **TERRORISM**
AROUND THE WORLD.

ARMY RANGERS TRAIN TO PARACHUTE
OUT OF A PLANE TO HELP GET TO WHERE
THEY ARE NEEDED MOST.

LEADING THE WAY

Since 1944, the motto of the U.S. Army Rangers has been "Rangers lead the way!" This stands true today! With just 18 hours notice, each Ranger battalion is capable of reaching faraway locations to complete covert missions.

When the Ranger battalions were established in 1974, General Creighton Abrams, Army Chief of Staff, said he wanted the Rangers to be the best of the army and a model for the rest of the army. Besides being physically strong, Rangers would be smart, tough, and courageous. This combination of qualities is what makes the Army Rangers an elite fighting force.

MILITARY LEADERS BELIEVE THAT CONFLICTS
WILL BE SMALLER IN THE FUTURE AND THAT
THE NEED FOR HIGHLY TRAINED TROOPS LIKE
THE RANGERS WILL BE GREATER.

allied: Referring to the countries that came together to defeat Germany, Italy, and Japan during World War II.

battalion: A large organized group of soldiers.

commando: A soldier who is trained to carry out surprise attacks on an enemy.

covert: Made or done secretly.

elite: Superior in talent and ability.

guerrilla: Having to do with methods of war that include covert operations, such as small teams, reconnaissance, and secret attacks against an enemy.

invade: To enter an area to take control by military force.

mission: A specific task a person or group is asked to complete.

reconnaissance: Military activity in which soldiers are sent to find out information about an enemy.

recruit: A new member of a military force. Also, to invite people to join a military force.

terrain: A type of land in an area.

terrorism: The use of violence to scare people as a way of achieving a political goal.

volunteer: A person who offers to do something.

BOOKS

Lusted, Marcia Amidon. *Missions of the U.S. Army Rangers.* Troy, MI: Momentum Press, 2016.

Slater, Lee. *Army Rangers.* Minneapolis, MN: ABDO, 2016.

WEBSITES

How the Army Rangers Work

science.howstuffworks.com/army-ranger.htm
Learn much more about the Army Rangers here.

U.S. Army Rangers

www.army.mil/ranger
Visit the official website for the Army Rangers to learn more about what they do.

INDEX